I love this fascinating and compelling sequence that utilises the unique dynamic of tan-tenga to travel the distance between poetry and science, in order to close in on new connections that can themselves cross freely, over the border, between detonating knowledge and imploding language. The instinctive juxtapositions here engage the expansive promise of the minimal to produce something like a series of mental diamonds that glisten like water droplets interspersed on a string.

Tim Allen
Author of *The Indescribable Thrill of the Half-Volley*

Travel through hyperloops and Fermi bubbles as Ashraf and Thomas explore space, virtual reality, artificial intelligence, and the future of the self in *Infinity Strings*, an ambitious collection of tan-renga by two outstanding poets. It is an extension of the speculative genres, where the tired images of traditional verse are replaced by imagined futures grounded in the potential realities of technological advancement. *Infinity Strings* is a speculative gem that even H. G. Wells and Isaac Asimov themselves could have approved. It is a consequential contribution to the genre that will encourage others to continue testing the boundaries of the form.

M. R. Defibaugh
Former Editor of the *Tan-Renga Chapbook Series*

Welcome to the virtual existences of alternative and future universes. Within the art and science of *Infinity Strings* Hifsa Ashraf and R.C. Thomas weave words and spatial imagery into phenomena that spark in and out of reality. This is a book of experiment and invention, traveling deep into the core of lived and imagined experience. Whether in outer-space, inner-space or cyberspace, these are journeys you will want to take on with mind, body and soul.

John Hawkhead
Author of *Four Horse Parable*

A remarkable collection of tan-renga:

'Before there was renga with many links there was the renga form of only two parts . . . if it takes two persons to write it's called a tan renga—short linked elegance'—School of Renga (Jane Reichhold 1937-2016)

There's also the gift of a glossary: I just had to look up one word that means 'placebo pill', though I read it a different way (at least in my head).

The human race is explored in a wonderful prosperity of play intermingled by serious thought: Hifsa Ashraf and R.C. Thomas have cracked time tourism!

Alan Summers
Founder of *Call of the Page*

Hifsa Ashraf is an award-winning bilingual poet, author, editor, and social activist from Rawalpindi, Pakistan. She is a pioneer in her country for writing modern Japanese-style micropoetry in English and Urdu. Her work has been widely published in international journals, newspapers, magazines, blogs and anthologies. As an editor, she jointly curates the Haiku Commentary blog. Hifsa is the author of six micropoetry books on gender-based taboos, prejudice, stereotyping, mental health, cultural symbolism, cultural history, women's rights and empowerment, children's rights, interfaith harmony, climate change, socio-cultural, and socio-political issues. She won The Touchstone Award for Individual Poems 2021 from The Haiku Foundation, USA, her poem was shortlisted for The Touchstone Award for Individual Poems 2022, and she received an honourable mention for her poetry collection, *Her Fading Henna Tattoo*, in the Touchstone Distinguished Books Award 2020 and in the Haiku Society of America Merit Book Award 2021. Her most recent micropoetry collection is *hazy crescent moon* (2022) by Alba Publishing UK.

Web: hifsays.blogspot.com
Social: hifsays

R.C. Thomas lives in Plymouth, UK. His poetry collections, *The Strangest Thankyou* (2012) and *Zygote Poems* (2015) were published by Cultured Llama under the name Richard Thomas. *Faunistics: A Collection of Wild Haiku and Illustrations* (2024) was published independently. He edited Symmetry Pebbles, was Creative Writing editor for Tribe, co-edited Thief, and was Managing Editor of INK, Plymouth University's creative writing journal. He was shortlisted for the Touchstone Awards for Individual Poems in 2022, received joint first place in the Sharpening the Green Pencil Haiku Contest 2022, first place in the Third Maya Lyubenova Haiku Contest, had a 'Selected Haiku Submission' in the 13th Yamadera Basho Memorial Museum English Haiku Contest, and was selected as one of the 'Top Creative Haiku Authors' in Europe in 2021 and 2022 consecutively.

Web: rcthomasthings.com
Etsy: etsy.com/uk/shop/RCThomasThings
Social: rcthomasthings

INFINITY STRINGS
HIFSA ASHRAF & R.C. THOMAS

Tan-renga
(linked verse)

Regular verses by Hifsa Ashraf
Italic verses by R.C. Thomas

Original photographs by Hifsa Ashraf
Illustrations and photo-editing by R.C. Thomas

First edition published in 2025 by Infinity Books

A CIP record for this book is available from The British
Library

ISBN 978-1-3999-9308-1

Original photographs by Hifsa Ashraf

www.hifsays.blogspot.com

Photo-editing, illustration, cover design and layout by R.C.
Thomas

www.rcthomasthings.com

For the threshold between mankind
and artificial intelligence

CONTENTS

PREFACE

Modernity is in full swing and the world is transforming. New phenomena arise constantly, taking their hold on society. Science and technology advances at a rapid pace. This is the reality we live in. This is our existence and survival. Our curiosity to explore beyond the box of being human is leading us down an artificially intelligent road. Can our curiosity unlock the universe's secrets? Will it unveil a utopia we don't want to leave or a nightmare we can't escape? Our imaginations rule the roost. Our perspectives broaden. We are entering a new world. But at what cost?

Written by two poets from very different parts of the world, using modern communication devices so often called into question here, *Infinity Strings* is a book of tan-renga, a collaborative Japanese form of poetry finding its roots in haikai. Here, our past, present and future as a human race are explored, aware that what might be difficult to comprehend today may be trivial come tomorrow. From tradition to progression; from simplicity to complexity; from being to becoming, these poems touch on obvious and subtle changes in society, as fathomable as they are unfathomable. This is a tour of two parallel worlds co-existing inside and outside of us. This is what we can see. This is what we can't see.

Hifsa Ashraf *& R.C. Thomas*

aurora
stepping out
of the primordial self

an Oculus
sunrise

Chicxulub impact
space between us
opening up

the Pandora's box
of here and now

slowly shifting
the last bit of weight
a s t e r o i d   b e l t

blinking stars
around the irises

mirror illusion
dividing the self
into bits and bites

poisoned
eating apples

gone in a flash
the moment
we keep

a hyperloop
of impulses

satellite saturation
compressing
to safe space

calling through
interference

new subscriber
what follows
is emptiness

VPN proxy
fixing narratives

echolocation
rifts in the mountain
shifting gravity

our DMs begin
to ping pong

Carina Nebula
relapsing pulses
ash clouds

young stars
at our peak

Oberonian
with age
the pock marks
                    deepen

the abyss
of a night mirage

meteor shower
the beliefs we hold
back

Fukitol
compounding our fate

tracking algorithm
on the solar panel
midnight stars

*dreams burned
into sleep*

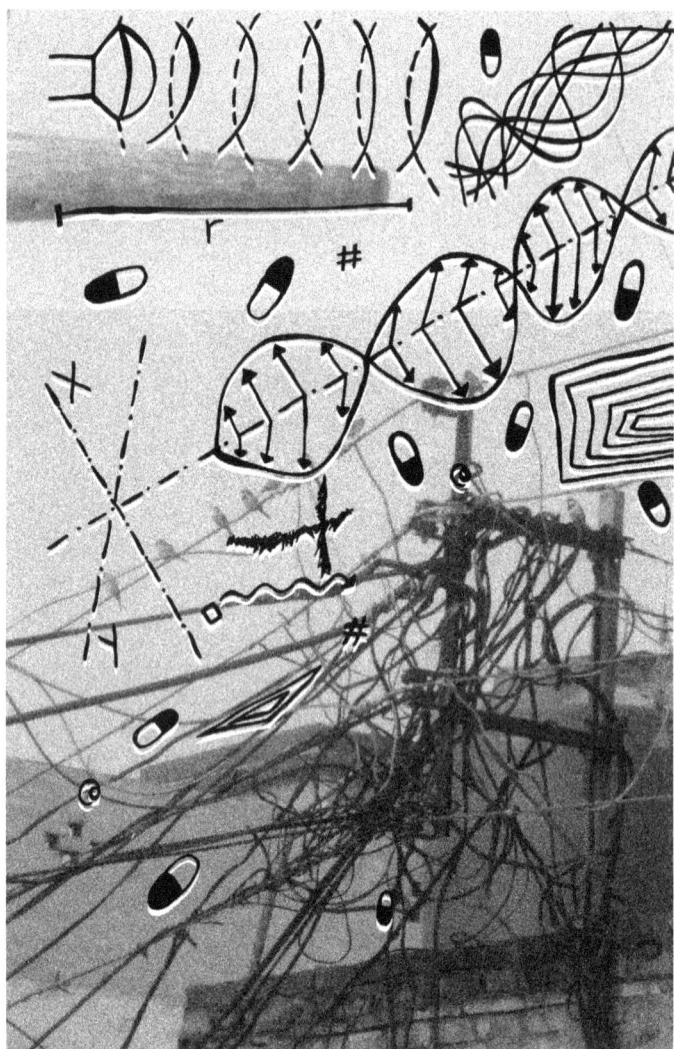

molten mantle
our burns reveal
what's cooled

split view
disrupting dopamine

resetting
personal battles
optical field

from petahertz
       *bloom exa***hertz**

trapped in
the blatant lies
greenhouse effect

*tired of turning it
off and on*

this period
of oscillation
full stop ●

jumbling up
the digital rhetoric

cyber attack
bugs swarm
the data network

reprogramming
our inner moth

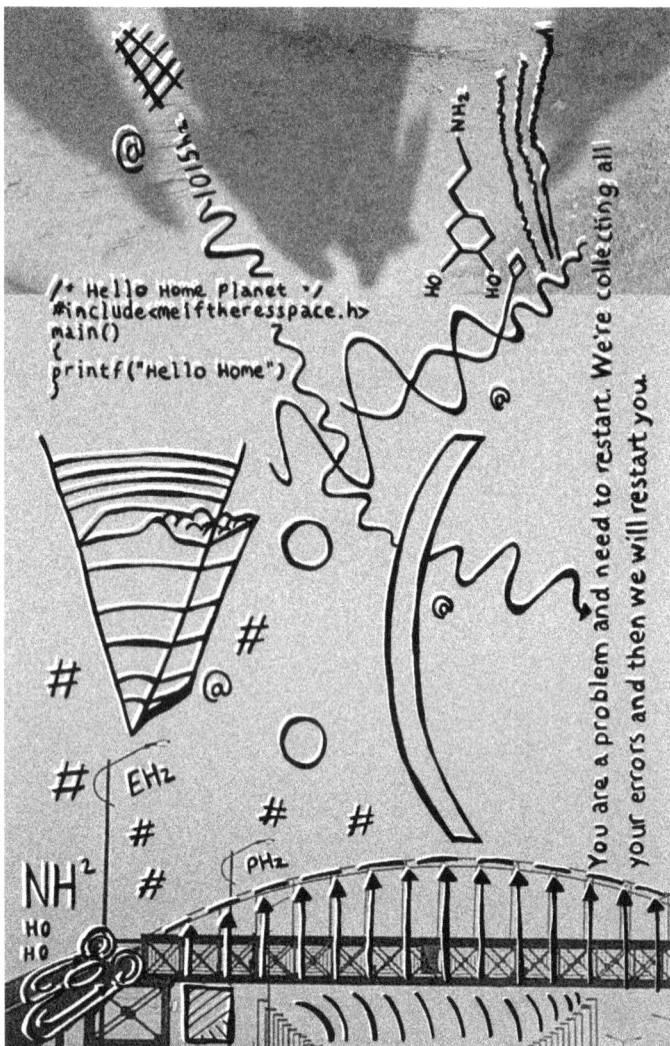

hoverboard
how clueless
the final destiny

1ᴜᴘ
for another try

squeezing
between two worlds
Fermi bubbles

back home
in just a click

where altitude
meets azimuth
moot point

a perfect parabola
of wishes

channeling
the same thoughts
lobotomy TV

white noise
cutting through receptors

brain fog
gliding through the mist
a robotic goose

a bird in the hand
out of memory

storm brewing
a hyperobject enters
the group chat

juggling with
the emojis

blind spot
AI's reality
differs from mine

drowning in
the vortex of neon

doomscrolling
bad news
until

the

very

end

refolding
an old paper crane

caching nightmares
what's left of now
kept for later

catalysing
phosphenes

inertial mass
pushing back
increased charges

for a split second
blackout

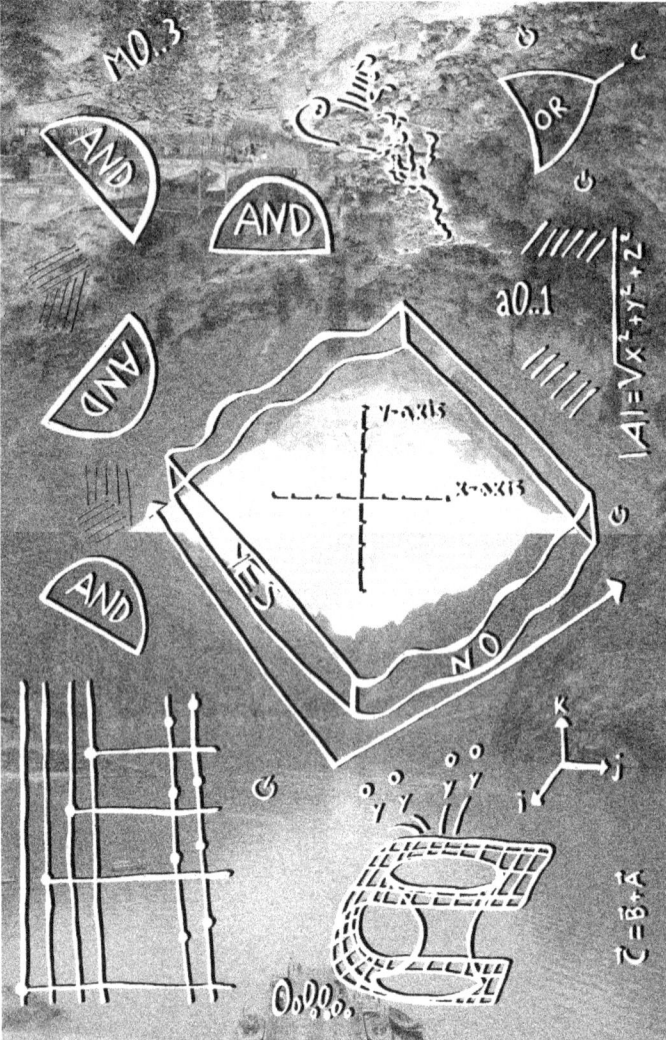

NO.3

AND

AND

OR

a0.1

AND

$|A| = \sqrt{x^2 + y^2 + z^2}$

AND

y-axis

x-axis

YES

NO

AND

k

j

i

$\vec{C} = \vec{B} + \vec{A}$

$O_0 O_1 O_2$

dark energy
still wandering
the Milky Way

*our hooded cloaks
worn thin*

c0ld w1nd
the f0ne v1brates
w1v every msg

dec1pher1ng
the b1nary c0des

monotone talk
the bumpy road
through Airpods

hearing aids...

nothing

centripetal chatter
missed points
come back around

thoughts turning
to molecular clouds

crypto autumn
the $s_n{}_a k^e s_k i^n$ clings
to bare feet

treading carefully
where it counts the most

exoplanets
tracing back
a mutual connection

who requests
whose request

twitching mice
following you
following me

sinking in
the ChatGPT

worl...   wi...   ...eb
this buffering
our buffering

counting on
the free particles

James Webb
where do you fall
on life's spectrum

landing converted
in the rushes

screenshots
doubling up
our weary frame rate

chroma keying
another shapeshifter

vertigo spiral
blending shadows
with delusions

all over screens
our projected ascent

isotopic abundance
egos reach
their points

an ellipsis
leaves   space   for   more

heads in the cloud
making   room
for other migraines

Starlink amplifying
source codes

raster image
camouflaging
our past

freedom
in another dimension

terraforming
last season's house plant
finds new life

round the clock
clearing doubts

guilty pleasure
on the snooze
self-talk

resetting
for tomorrow's tomorrow

parallel Jupiters
orbiting
our whispers

the pull and push
of zero gravity

3D flooring
losing balance
to the black hole

escalator

      to

        the

           stomach

drop by drop
breaking down
a caffeine kick

molecules dance
with nerves

night shift
a wired interface poses
for the sun

replugging
our cognitive module

dolphin chronotype
I surf
at high tide

ASMR
page click by page click

solving
the pixelated image
hi-tech zone

tutorial
on a broken link

photosynthesis
resetting
a tainted aura

progress update
overshared

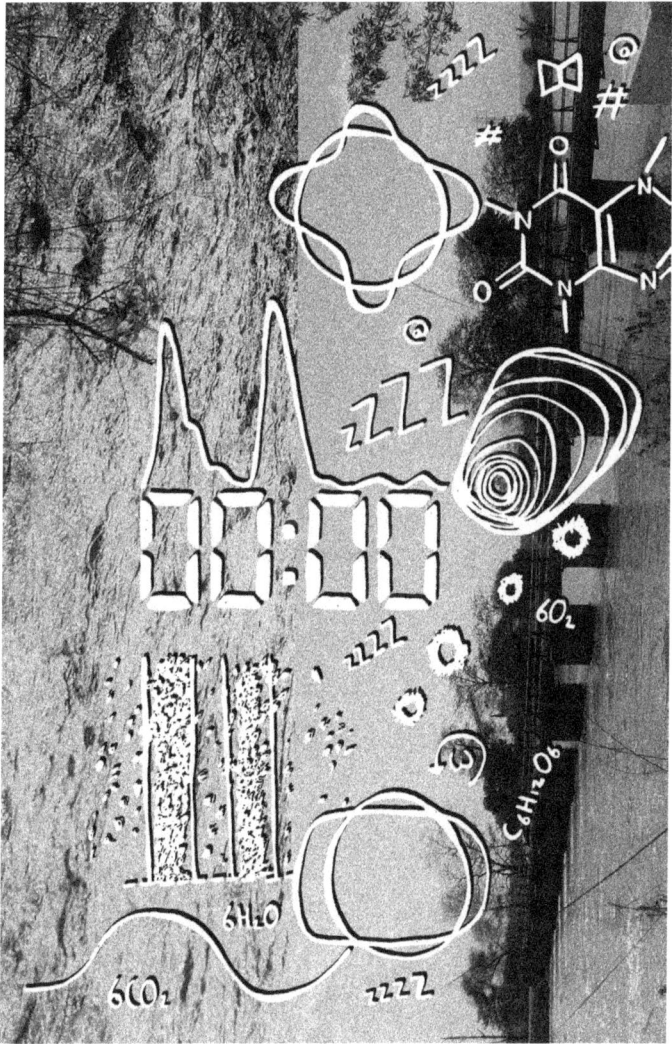

situationship
subtle feelings still
in a vacuum

#mindovermatter
#followyourheart

selfie vector
tilting towards
Cepheus

install:
scalar.exe

absolute zero
strands of gray curl
around the temples

*updating social media
images*

imposing stories
added by AI
after the fact

concussion
through the filter

existential thought
at the heart of it
Cygnus X-1

unraveling
the gravitational waves

our fleeting moment
in the spotlight
gamma ray

aggravating
corneal abrasion

letting off steam
our lotus tries
the autoclave

optimizing
inner demons

normalising
the microstructure
we fire up again

at ground zero
celestial bodies

data mining
all differences
buried

the hatchet
up for grabs

Fermi estimate
the whole atom bomb
is theirs

boosting up
brain nebula

you leave
no, you leave
geostationary satellite

out of the blue
this weightless argument

final judgment
screams dilute
the darkness

emitting us only
LEDs

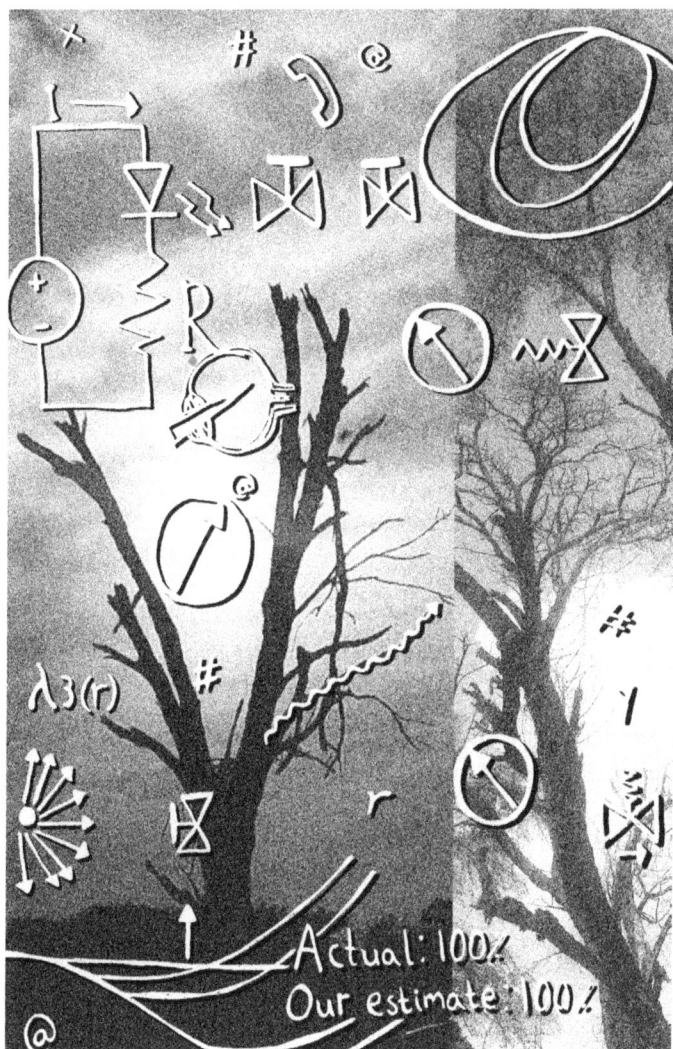
Actual: 100%
Our estimate: 100%

GLOSSARY

3D flooring: A technique that uses high resolution images in the flooring for a three-dimensional effect.

Asteroid belt: A torus-shaped belt in the solar system between the orbits of Mars and Jupiter.

ASMR: Autonomous Sensory Meridian Response. A sensation that involves personal but pleasant responses to specific stimuli.

Autoclave: A device or a machine used for the sterilization of objects.

Azimuth: The angle measured between north on the observer's horizon and a celestial body.

Caching: The temporary storage of computer data.

Carina Nebula: A large and immense cloud in our milky way with dense gas and dust.

Centripetal: Centripetal force causes an object to continue moving along a curved path.

Cepheus: A constellation in the northern hemisphere named after King Cepheus of Aethiopia.

Chicxulub impact: The Chicxulub crater is an asteroid impact crater buried beneath the Yucatán Peninsula in Mexico.

Chroma keying: A technique which uses specific visual effects and colours to produce desired background images.

Cognitive modules: A systematic computerized model of problem-solving by focusing on cognitive processes.

Corneal abrasion: A scratch or injury on the surface of the eye.

Crypto: Cryptocurrency is a digital currency that doesn't depend on banks or monetary authorities.

Cygnus X-1: A galactic x-ray source and black hole found in the constellation Cygnus.

Data mining: The process of extracting information from raw data to help identify and resolve issues.

Dark energy: An unknown negative energy opposing the effects of gravity, affecting the universe and its existence, and stretching the fabric of spacetime.

Dolphin chronotype: A characteristic of people who struggle to fall and stay asleep at night and who feel tired during the day.

Doomscrolling: Spending an excessive amount of time scrolling through social media, news, videos, etc, online, often in pursuit of negative information.

Echolocation: The process of using the reflection of sound to locate objects.

Exahertz: A very large unit of frequency equal to one quintillion hertz. *See Petahertz.*

Exoplanets: A planet which orbits a star outside of the solar system.

Fermi bubbles: Two large orbs of gas and cosmic rays which exist above and below the Galactic centre.

Fermi estimate: A method used for simplifying complex problems based on rough estimation.

Free particles: A particle with no bound or limited field.

Fukitol: A placebo pill to alter behaviour patterns and improve health.

Gamma ray: Emitted from atomic nuclei, gamma rays have the shortest wavelength electromagnetic waves and highest energy.

Geostationary satellite: Appearing stationary from Earth as it rotates and spins in the same direction, making one full rotation in twenty-four hours.

Gravitational waves: High intensity waves which cause ripples in spacetime.

Greenhouse effect: The process through which heat is trapped by gases in the atmosphere, warming the planet.

Hyperloop: A high-speed shuttle service for both passengers and freight.

Hyperobject: An object with vitality that cannot be touched. For example, climate change, race, or class.

Inertial mass: The mass of a body as determined by its momentum, as opposed to gravitational mass.

Isotopic abundance: The quantity of isotopes of elements found in nature.

LED: An electronic device which emits light when a voltage is applied to it.

Lobotomy: A surgical procedure used for psychological and neurological disorders, in which the frontal lobe is severed from different parts of the brain.

Microstructure: Small scale structures which are only visible with an optical microscope.

Molecular clouds: An interstellar cloud cool enough to allow hydrogen to pass up into hydrogen molecules.

Oberonian: Relating to Oberon, the outermost moon of Uranus.

Oculus: A circular, round, or oval shaped opening, i.e., a human eye. Also, a virtual reality headset.

Optical field: A vectorial field made up of five parameters: amplitude, phase, frequency, polarisation and state of polarisation (SOP).

Petahertz: A very large unit of electrical frequency equivalent to one quadrillion hertz. See *Exahertz.*

Phosphenes: A sensation of a ring or spot of light produced by pressure on the eyeball, or direct stimulation of the visual system other than by light.

Raster image: A two-dimensional image composed of pixels.

Sagittarius A: The supermassive blackhole at the centre of the Milky Way.

Scalar.exe: In computing, a repository management tool which configures advanced Git settings, maintains repositories in the background and reduces data sent across the network.

Situationship: A romantic relationship deemed more than being friends but which remains undefined/free of commitment.

Source codes: A set of computing codes consisting of information and data written by a programmer.

Terraforming: A hypothetical process of normalising the atmosphere of a planet to make it habitable.

Undecillion: A number equal to 1 followed by 36 zeros (US); a number equal to 1 followed by 66 zeros (British).

Vector: A digital image which places lines and shapes in a two-dimensional or three-dimensional space, and has been created using a sequence of mathematical statements.

VPN proxy: A proxy server which uses a remote server to keep IP addresses hidden and encrypted.

James Webb: The James Webb Space Telescope (JWST) is a telescope used for infrared astronomy.

ACKNOWLEDGEMENTS

A special thanks to the editors and publishers of the following publications in which present or earlier versions of some of these poems previously appeared:

autumn wind tan-renga anthology (ed. Matthew Defibaugh), Die Leere Mitte, Failed Haiku, Frogpond, Heliosparrow, Lothlorien Poetry Journal, Noon: Journal of the Short Poem, Otoliths, Petrichor, Prune Juice, Wales Haiku Journal.

Thanks, also, to all family, friends, editors, and poets who have and who will directly or indirectly support us and contribute to this book in any way.